STO

Nuclear fuel

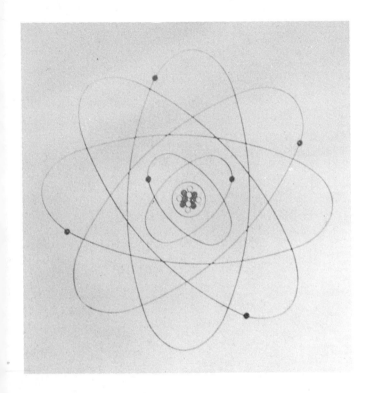

Nuclear fuel plays an ever-increasing part in satisfying the demands of our energy-hungry world. The continued use of nuclear energy is, however, a fiercely debated subject. Virtually every day opposing views are voiced in the newspapers.

This book is not *for* or *against* the use of nuclear fuel. It describes *how* the energy locked in the nuclei of uranium atoms is released under controlled conditions, and how it is generated into nuclear power. This complicated process is explained in clear and simple language by the author, who has spent many years working on the development of nuclear fuel.

The book has nearly one hundred illustrations, and is the ideal introduction – for both children and adults – to perhaps the most crucial development of the twentieth century. It will be particularly useful to the science teacher who wishes to show how developments in physics, mathematics and chemistry have a practical use in determining the way we live today, and the way we are likely to live.

NUCLEAR FUEL

C.A. MANN

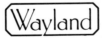

World Resources Series

Timber
Rubber
Iron and Steel
Sugar
Seafood
Oil
Gas
Coal
Cocoa, Tea and Coffee
Grain

Meat
Nuclear Fuel
Gold and Silver
Soya
Alternative Energy
Cotton
Wool
Tobacco
Rice
Copper

Frontispiece *The twentieth-century landscape – an atomic reactor in the U.S.A.*

ISBN 0 85078 250 3
© Copyright 1979 Wayland Publishers Limited
First published in 1979 by
Wayland Publishers Limited
49 Lansdowne Place, Hove
East Sussex, BN3 1HF, England

Phototypeset by Computacomp (UK) Ltd.
Fort William, Scotland
Printed and bound in Great Britain by
The Pitman Press, Bath, England.

Contents

The new source of energy

Early in the 1950s, a new kind of electricity generating station was planned and built – the nuclear power station. In Great Britain today, one eighth of the electricity generated is done so by nuclear power. This fraction will increase as more nuclear power stations are built.

Other countries are also beginning to rely upon nuclear power to generate electricity. In Europe it is used in Belgium, Czechoslovakia, Finland, France, Italy, the Netherlands, Spain, Sweden, Switzerland, West Germany and the USSR. In North America it is used in Canada, the USA and Mexico. In South America it is used in Argentina. In Asia it is used in India, Pakistan, South Korea and Taiwan.

Fifty years ago no one knew how to release nuclear energy, and few people even believed it would be possible. Now it is a source of power upon which the world is likely to become increasingly dependent. What is the nuclear fuel which is used to generate electricity? To answer this question we need to explain what is meant by the words "energy", "power", and "fuel".

Left   *The building of a new era – the Bruce nuclear power station in Canada under construction early in the 1970s.*

Above   *More and more electricity is likely to be generated by nuclear power in the future.*

Energy

When we call something a "fuel", we mean that we can use it to produce energy. We use the word energy in everyday talk – we call lively people "full of energy". Scientists use the word with a more exact meaning. They mean "the ability to do work" or "the ability to cause things to change".

Energy changes objects by making them hotter, making them move faster, lifting them against the Earth's pull (gravity), or by changing their chemical composition. Energy never disappears, though it can change its form. If you heat some water, perhaps by burning fuel to release energy as heat, the hot water will pass its heat to other things it touches. It may make the air above it move. If you push a ball and start it moving so that it hits another one, it will start that one moving as well, slowing down as it loses energy itself. Scientists say that energy is "conserved", meaning that it can change its form but is never lost.

Left *Energy never disappears, though it can change its form. Energy is here passed from one ball to another.*

Above *James Watt, the Scottish engineer who made the first efficient steam engine.*

The modern unit of energy is the "joule", so-called in memory of James Joule, the Englishman who first showed that heat is a form of energy. He lived from 1818 to 1889. We use the word "power" to mean the rate at which we are using or releasing energy. Power is measured in watts. One watt equals one joule per second. Here we are remembering James Watt (1736–1819), the Scottish engineer who made the first efficient steam engine.

Use of energy

After scientists and engineers had learnt how to measure energy, their work became easier. They realized that heat, movement, chemical changes, electric currents and so on were all forms of energy, and their understanding of the world became clearer. It also became more interesting and exciting.

Engineers learnt how to make use of the various forms of energy. They discovered how to harness energy from fire and other chemical reactions. When people began to make use of engines in workshops and mines, they were using more energy than before. They had formerly relied on their own muscle power, or the power of animals. The rich man had been able to get his work done by using the energy of servants or slaves. Today, if we have good supplies of energy, we can get the same work done by pressing a switch. Through Man's ability to harness energy, the world has become a kinder place to live in. Most people have more goods and greater comfort.

Unfortunately, people have also learnt how to destroy things more easily by using new sources of energy. Energy can be harnessed by Man for good things or bad.

Left *The energy of running water was once used to turn the wheel of this old mill.*

Above *Before engineers learnt how to make use of other forms of energy, the only energy harnessed was that of animals.*

11

Sources of energy – the Sun

All our energy comes from the Sun or from the Earth. The Sun pours energy on to the Earth, and we see it as light and feel it as heat. The Sun's rays heat the water of the seas, and some of the water evaporates. The air containing water vapour is heated and moves about as winds. The winds blow over the land, droplets

Above *As long ago as 1882 people were making machines run with solar energy.*

of water form clouds, and then fall as rain. The rain runs back to the sea as rivers.

Plants change some of the Sun's light into chemical energy, storing it in their leaves and stems. We eat plants, or other animals that have eaten plants. The energy is released in the heat of our bodies and the power of our muscles. We can burn some plants to release heat directly. Coal is the remains of plants which grew many millions of years ago. Oil and gas are the remains of ancient animal life. This is why coal, oil and gas are sometimes called "fossil fuels". When we burn them we are releasing the

Above *Coal being burnt to manufacture gas in 1878.*

Above *'Fire' – when we burn something we are indirectly releasing the energy of the Sun.*

energy which came from the Sun to the Earth millions of years ago. All these sources of energy come directly or indirectly from the Sun. Sunshine itself is the direct source of energy. Windpower, water power, coal, oil, gas, and human and animal muscle power come indirectly from the Sun.

13

Above   *The inside of the Earth is hot because of the radioactivity of some of the elements it contains. Heat energy causes mud to boil.*

Sources of energy – the Earth

Our other sources of energy are from the Earth. The energy of the tides comes from the rotation of the Earth, and the gravitational pull of the Moon and the Sun. If we harness tidal energy, we are using some of the energy the Earth has had since it was formed. The inside of the Earth is hot, because of the radioactivity of some of the elements it contains. Even though the Earth was very hot when it was first formed, the inside would have cooled long ago if not for this radioactivity.

Some of the heat energy from inside the Earth is carried to the surface in hot springs of water. This heat can be used directly, or be obtained by drilling into the Earth. Finally, we now know how to release energy from some of the radioactive elements which have been in the Earth since it was formed. This nuclear fuel, as it is called, is the subject of the rest of this book.

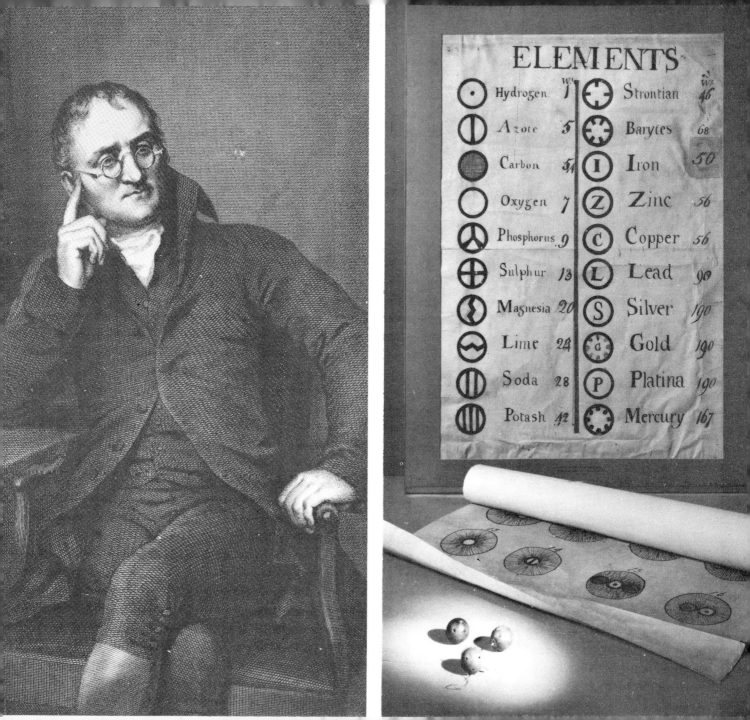

ELEMENTS·

		w.				W.
⊙	Hydrogen	1	⊕	Strontian		46
⦶	Azote	5	✳	Barytes		68
⬤	Carbon	54	Ⓘ	Iron		50
◯	Oxygen	7	Ⓩ	Zinc		56
⧆	Phosphorus	9	Ⓒ	Copper		56
⊕	Sulphur	13	Ⓛ	Lead		90
◑	Magnesia	20	Ⓢ	Silver		190
◯	Lime	24	Ⓖ	Gold		190
⦶	Soda	28	Ⓟ	Platina		190
⦶	Potash	42	✳	Mercury		167

Atoms

Matter – every solid object, liquid and gas – is made up of atoms. You can break things up into smaller and smaller pieces, but an atom is the smallest ordinary piece that there can be. (As we shall see, atoms too can be broken into parts, but only by special forces.) The Greek philosopher Democritus, who lived about 2300 years ago, guessed that matter was made up of atoms. The first scientist to work out a modern atomic theory was John Dalton, who lived in Britain from 1766 to 1844. Dalton realized that chemistry could be explained more easily if atoms of different elements have different weights.

Atoms are very small – a grain of salt a millimetre across contains over twenty million million million atoms. Air is a mixture of oxygen, nitrogen, and some other gases. The oxygen atoms and the nitrogen atoms are

Far left *John Dalton – the first scientist to work out a modern atomic theory.*
Left *Dalton realized that atoms of different elements have different weights.*

Above *The size of the atom – each grain of salt to the left of this coin contains over twenty million million million atoms!*

linked in pairs, called molecules. Two oxygen atoms form an oxygen molecule, and two nitrogen atoms form a nitrogen molecule. Each different sort of atom is called an "element". There are about a hundred elements, and all substances are made up of molecules – compounds of some or other of the elements. Some materials are made up of atoms of one element – copper, iron, gold, carbon and sulphur are elements, for example.

17

Atoms and radioactivity

By about 1900, chemists had discovered more than eighty different elements, and knew that everything was made up of mixtures or compounds of them. (They realized that there might be some rare elements which had not been discovered yet.) The weights of atoms of different elements could be compared. Scientists found that many elements had "atomic weights" which were multiples of the atomic weight of the lightest element, hydrogen. Carbon atoms were twelve times as heavy as hydrogen atoms, for example, and oxygen atoms were sixteen times heavier. Some atomic weights didn't fit into this pattern, but enough

Above *A balloon rises because it is filled with hydrogen which is lighter than air.*

did to suggest that the heavier atoms might be built up from the lighter ones.

It was then discovered that some elements – the heaviest ones – were slowly changing all the time. They were giving off rays as they did so, and were therefore called "radioactive". The Polish scientist Marie Sklodowska, helped by her French husband Pierre Curie, showed that uranium, the heaviest element, slowly changed into other elements. She discovered the element which she called "polonium" after her native country. She went on to discover more elements. The best known of these is radium.

Above *Marie Curie discovered that some elements were radioactive.*

Above *Some materials, like gold, are made up of atoms of the same element. The atomic weight of gold is 190 times more than that of hydrogen. But even gold is not as heavy as uranium.*

The nucleus of the atom

If atoms could change in this way, scientists realized that they could not be simple particles, but must have a structure and parts. The New Zealand scientist Ernest Rutherford (1871–1937) discovered that each atom has a central core – a nucleus. This nucleus, although a thousand times smaller than the whole atom, contains most of the weight (mass) of the atom.

Above *Ernest Rutherford was the first scientist to discover that each atom has a central core – the nucleus.*

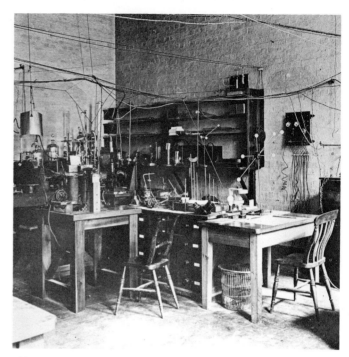

Above *Rutherford's research room.*

The nucleus is made up of two kinds of particles. One sort are protons, which carry a positive electric charge. The others are neutrons, which weigh the same but carry no charge – they are "neutral". Round the nucleus are electrons in orbit. They are negatively charged, and balance the charges of the protons. The size of the atom is the size of the orbits of the electrons. The nucleus is in the centre of the atom like the sun is in the centre of our solar system of planets.

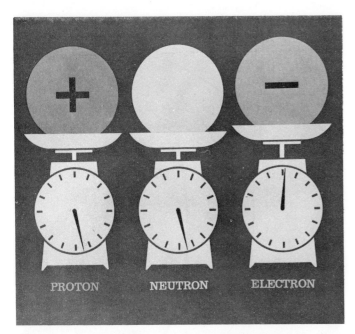

Above *The composition and weight of an atom. Protons carry a positive electric charge. Neutrons weigh the same but carry no charge. Electrons are negative.*

Atoms of different elements have different numbers of protons and neutrons in their nuclei. The nucleus of the lightest atom, hydrogen, has only one proton. The next heaviest element, helium, has two protons and two neutrons. It therefore weighs four times as much as hydrogen. Uranium has 92 protons and over 140 neutrons. A radioactive element changes into another element when protons leave the nucleus.

When scientists measured the energies re-leased through radioactive changes in elements like uranium and radium, they found them to be very large. The nucleus contains much more energy than the electrons in orbit around it. Chemical energy comes from changes in the electrons, so could it be possible to get energy from nuclear changes? Rutherford himself thought that it was not possible.

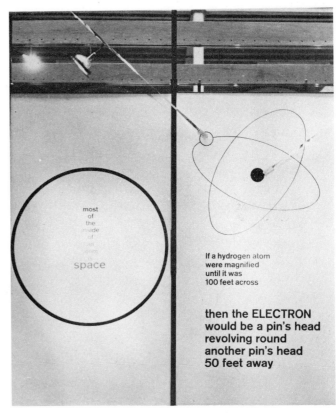

most of the inside of an atom is space

If a hydrogen atom were magnified until it was 100 feet across

then the ELECTRON would be a pin's head revolving round another pin's head 50 feet away

Fission

In 1932, the British scientist James Chadwick showed that neutrons could be shot out of nuclei and be studied on their own. Many people experimented on the effects of neutrons on other atoms. Because they are neutral, neutrons are not affected by the electric charges of nuclei, and can be shot into them. When a neutron enters a nucleus it can make it radioactive, and it may change it into another element.

When uranium, the heaviest element, was bombarded with neutrons the results were puzzling. The German scientists Otto Hahn and Lise Meitner were the first to see what must be happening. The uranium nucleus was not just absorbing a neutron. It was splitting into two, forming two atoms, each about half the weight of a uranium atom. They called this process "fission", from the Latin word meaning to split.

A large amount of energy was released. Not only that, but the atom gave off some more neutrons as it split. If these neutrons could in turn cause other uranium atoms nearby to split, scientists realized that uranium could be a practical source of very large amounts of energy.

Right *Otto Hahn. Hahn and Lise Meitner were the first scientists to discover that an atom could be split.*

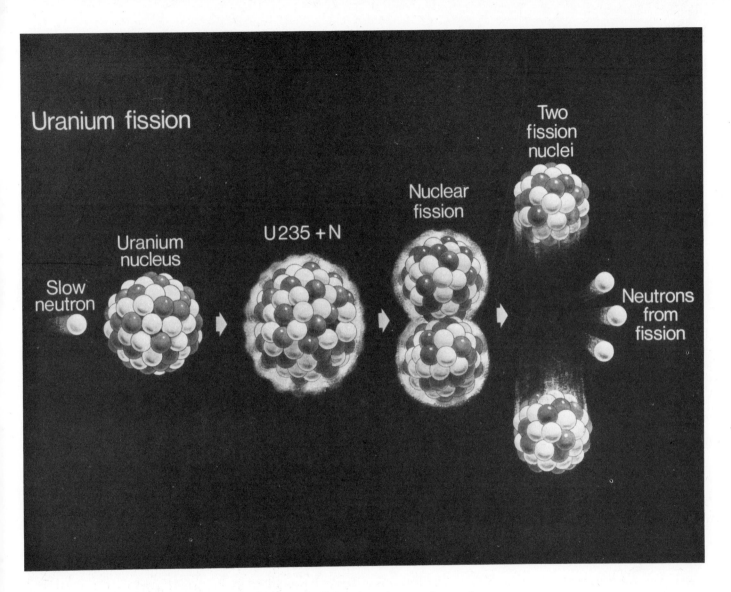

Uranium fission

Slow neutron

Uranium nucleus

U235 + N

Nuclear fission

Two fission nuclei

Neutrons from fission

Above   *The fission process in a uranium nucleus.*

Above *The chain reaction – one ball fired at a group of balls causes them all to move. When uranium was bombarded with neutrons, one nucleus split, and the neutrons it released caused further fissions, which in turn caused still more.*

24

The chain reaction

What was needed to release energy was a "chain reaction". One nucleus would split, the neutrons it released would cause further fissions and those would cause still more. This is similar to what happens in the chemical reaction we call "burning". We heat up a fuel until some of its atoms or molecules combine with oxygen and give off heat energy. This energy heats up nearby atoms and molecules, which react.

When uranium was studied, scientists realized that only one "isotope" could easily be split. Most elements have more than one sort of atom. All atoms of a particular element have the same number of protons in their nuclei, and therefore the same number of electrons round each nucleus. It is this number of electrons which fixes the chemical properties of an atom and makes it an atom of carbon, gold or uranium. But nuclei can have different numbers of neutrons and still be chemically the same. Their weights are different, of course, and so the atoms of different atomic weights are called the isotopes of the element.

The commonest isotope of uranium has 92 protons and 146 neutrons in its nucleus. It is called uranium 238, since $92 + 146 = 238$. The isotope which splits up most readily when a neutron enters it is uranium 235. It has 92 protons and 143 neutrons. Less than one

uranium atom in a hundred is a uranium 235 atom. The rest are uranium 238 atoms, which absorb neutrons without splitting, and prevent the chain reaction from going on.

Above *In the chemical reaction we call burning, some of the molecules and atoms in the fuel combine with oxygen to give off heat energy. This energy heats up the nearby atoms and molecules which react.*

Fission and moderation

It may seem at first sight that the uranium 235 atoms have to be separated from the uranium 238 atoms before a chain reaction can take place. Indeed, if this difficult operation is achieved, a chain reaction starts very easily. Scientists call atoms which are easy to split "fissile", and they call the amount of fissile material needed to start a chain reaction the "critical mass".

There is a way of achieving a chain reaction with ordinary uranium – "natural uranium" as it is called. The neutrons given off in fission are travelling fast. If they are slowed down they are more likely to split up the uranium 235 nuclei. This slowing down is called "moderation".

A substance which slows down neutrons passing through it, without absorbing many, is called a "moderator". To make a chain reaction, it is therefore necessary to build a structure with pieces of uranium interleaved with pieces of moderator. Water and carbon are good moderators.

The first man-made fission chain reaction was brought about by a team of scientists and engineers led by the Italian scientist Enrico Fermi. They built a "pile" of uranium and carbon (in the form of graphite) which "went critical" in a squash court at the University of Chicago, USA, in 1942.

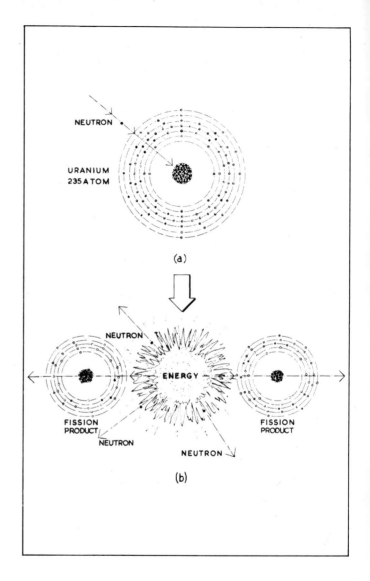

Above *How energy is released through fission.*

Enrichment

Uranium 235 and uranium 238 are the same chemically. Separating them is therefore very difficult. The ways in which it can be done depend on the small difference in weight between the two sorts of atom. Because of this difference the two sorts will not behave in quite the same way under some conditions.

Uranium is "enriched" as the compound uranium hexafluoride, which does not have to be heated much before it becomes a gas. If uranium hexafluoride is passed through plates in which there are many very small holes, the uranium 235 hexafluoride will come through slightly faster than the uranium 238 hexafluoride. This process of "diffusion" can be used, repeated many times, to produce two batches of material. In one there is a higher fraction of uranium 235 than there was at the beginning. This batch is "enriched". The other batch has a lower fraction of uranium 235, and is said to be "depleted".

Another enrichment process which has been developed recently uses centrifuges. These are containers which are spun very rapidly so that the heavier uranium 238 atoms move to the outer part.

Right *Enrico Fermi led the team which built the first atomic 'pile' of uranium and carbon in 1942.*

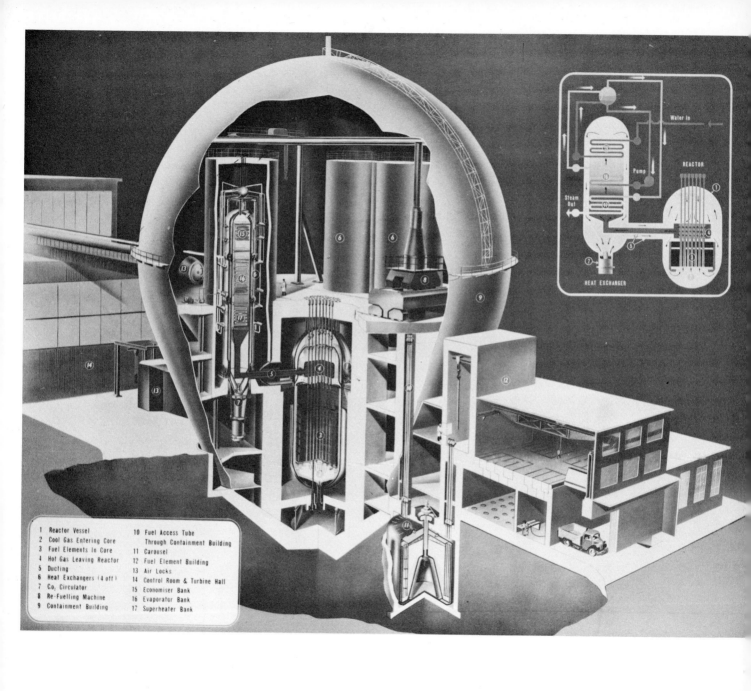

1 Reactor Vessel
2 Cool Gas Entering Core
3 Fuel Elements In Core
4 Hot Gas Leaving Reactor
5 Ducting
6 Heat Exchangers (4 off)
7 CO_2 Circulator
8 Re-Fuelling Machine
9 Containment Building
10 Fuel Access Tube
   Through Containment Building
11 Carousel
12 Fuel Element Building
13 Air Locks
14 Control Room & Turbine Hall
15 Economiser Bank
16 Evaporator Bank
17 Superheater Bank

Water in

REACTOR

Steam Out

Pump

HEAT EXCHANGER

Nuclear reactors

The first nuclear engineers called their assemblies "piles". Nowadays they are called "reactors". Most nuclear reactors are similar to the first one built in Chicago. There is a regular arrangement of "fuel elements" which contain the fissile material. Between the fuel elements there is usually a moderating material to slow down the neutrons. To regulate the reactor there are "control rods" sliding in channels through the reactor. These contain materials which absorb neutrons, and they are pushed in and out to control the power at which the reactor works. This central region of the reactor is often called the "core".

The fuel elements heat up as the uranium 235 atoms split up releasing energy. To extract the heat, a liquid or a gas is pumped through the core. This is called the "coolant". The hot coolant is arranged to give up its heat to boil water. The steam from the water passes through turbines. These in turn drive electric generators. The turbines and generators are similar to those you would find in a power station which gets its energy from burning coal or oil.

The core of a reactor is very radioactive. It is surrounded by a thick concrete shield which protects the people operating it.

Left *A diagram of an Advanced Gas-Cooled Reactor.*

Above *The turbine hall of a nuclear power station. These turbines are not unlike those found in a power station which generates electricity by burning coal or oil.*

Above   *Calder Hall in Great Britain was the first atomic power station to generate electricity.*

The first nuclear power stations

Fission had been discovered at the beginning of the Second World War and the first reactors were built to make plutonium for bombs. After the war, although military work went on, reactors to produce power for peaceful uses were designed and built. The first three to generate electricity were Calder Hall in Great Britain (1956), Shippingport in the USA (1957), and Troitsk in the Soviet Union (1958). All these reactors were quite small by modern standards, but they showed that nuclear power stations

Above *Nuclear reactors feed electricity into the power grid just as other stations do. In the U.S.S.R., all the power stations are united into a single system. This is the central control room of the integrated power system of Central Asia.*

were practicable. They fed electricity into the power "grid" just as other stations did, and they could be controlled easily. The amount of radioactivity they released was very small. In fact a power station burning coal may release more radioactivity into the air than a present-day nuclear station. This is because coal can contain very small amounts of uranium, which is released when the coal is burned.

31

Thermal reactors

Most of the power reactors built so far are of two main types. One uses graphite as the moderator and a gas, usually carbon dioxide, as the coolant. The earliest reactors built in Britain are called "Magnox" stations, after the alloy used for the fuel cans. The later ones are known as Advanced Gas-cooled Reactors (AGRs) and have uranium dioxide fuel sealed into cans.

The other main type uses water as both moderator and coolant. Water is not such a good moderator as graphite, but the chain reaction can still go on if the fuel is enriched. The water has to be put under pressure to raise its boiling point. A Pressurised Water Reactor (PWR) has the coolant circulating at a pressure 150 times that of the atmosphere. This hot water is used to boil another "circuit" of water to make the steam to drive the turbines. A Boiling Water Reactor (BWR) runs at a lower pressure so that the water boils as it leaves the core. This steam drives the turbines directly.

Above *The Pickering nuclear power station near Toronto, Canada is the largest nuclear power plant operating in the world. It generates enough electricity for a city of two million people.*

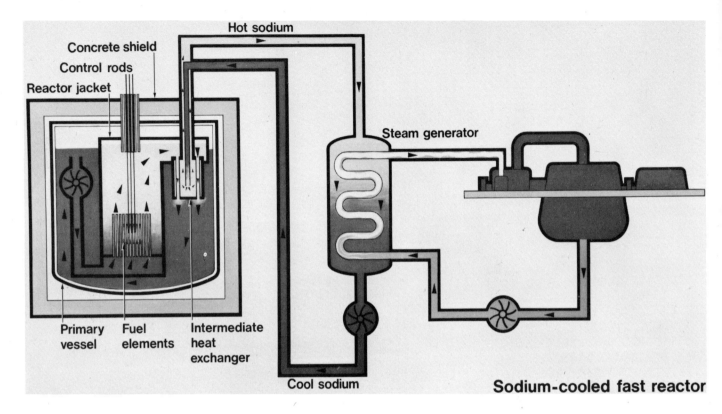

Labels in diagram:
- Concrete shield
- Control rods
- Reactor jacket
- Hot sodium
- Steam generator
- Primary vessel
- Fuel elements
- Intermediate heat exchanger
- Cool sodium

Sodium-cooled fast reactor

Fast reactors

All the reactors described so far use moderators to slow down the neutrons. A chain reaction can occur using fast neutrons, and without the need of a moderator. The fuel for this process needs to be either highly enriched uranium or plutonium, or a mixture of both. A reactor working in this way is called a "fast reactor". The fission processes are just the same as in a

thermal reactor, and it is controlled in the same way. "Fast" refers only to the speed of the neutrons used.

The reasons for building a fast reactor are two-fold. As well as producing power, like other reactors, it can also make fresh fuel. This it achieves by converting uranium 238, which cannot be used as fuel, to plutonium, which can.

34

Plutonium is fissile, uranium 238 is not. The core of a fast reactor can be surrounded by ordinary uranium. The fast neutrons flowing out of the core change some of the uranium to fissile plutonium. This can be extracted later and used as fuel.

Using uranium in thermal reactors, we can release less than one per cent of the energy in the uranium atoms. By converting it in fast reactors we should be able to release fifty times

Above *The fast reactor at Dounreay, Caithness, Scotland.*
as much energy from the same amount.

The core of a fast reactor has to be fairly small – about two metres (6·5 feet) across and one metre (3·2 feet) high. It is mounted in a tank of liquid sodium which is driven by pumps through channels in the core. A second sodium circuit extracts the heat which turns the water into steam. This steam is used, as in other reactors, to drive the turbines.

Uranium

Mining

Uranium is a white metal, denser even than lead. If you had a piece of aluminium weighing one kilogramme (2·2 lbs), a piece of steel the same size would weigh 2·8 kilogrammes (6·16 lbs), a piece of lead 4·2 kilogrammes (9·2 lbs) and a piece of uranium 7 kilogrammes (15·4 lbs). Like most metals, uranium is found in the earth, in deposits called ores.

There are uranium deposits in many parts of the world. The richest are in Canada, the USA, Czechoslovakia, Zaire and Namibia (Africa), and in Australia. Uranium ore is not usually very concentrated – there is often a lot of rock and other minerals mixed with the uranium compounds.

The extracted ore is ground into a powder and then dissolved in acid or other solutions. The uranium compounds, which form only a

Far left *Ore being shovelled into rail trucks before being taken to the surface.*
Left *At the surface the ore is crushed. This is the largest ore crusher in the world, capable of crushing 3,000 tonnes of ore an hour.*

Above *Drilling for uranium ore in Ontario, Canada.*

small part of the rock which has been dug out, can then be separated chemically. These separated compounds are called uranium ore concentrates. They contain 60 per cent or more of uranium, and can be transported to the refinery at a low cost.

Because uranium ore is not highly concentrated, the radioactivity it gives off is not very strong. What miners have to be protected against is the dust, for particles of uranium do harm to the lungs. Centuries ago, miners in Europe, digging ores which contained traces of uranium, saw that some mines caused "mountain sickness". This was lung cancer caused by breathing in the dust. All mines have to be well ventilated – uranium mines particularly so.

37

Above *A uranium hexafluoride cylinder is loaded for transportation to the diffusion plant.*

Refining

At the refinery, the uranium ore concentrate is ground up, and dissolved in nitric acid. The uranium goes through a series of chemical changes. It is turned to uranium trioxide by heating it, and then to another oxide, uranium dioxide. This is done by heating the trioxide with hydrogen. The dioxide is converted to uranium tetrafluoride, using hydrofluoric acid. It can then follow either one of two routes.

If we want uranium metal we react the tetrafluoride with magnesium metal. This uranium metal can then be made into the uranium rods for the Magnox reactor fuel elements.

Above *The control room in the fluidised bed plant at the Springfields Works near Preston, England.*

Most modern reactors use uranium dioxide fuel with the uranium enriched. To be enriched, the uranium needs to be in the form of the compound uranium hexafluoride. The uranium is enriched as hexafluoride, and is then converted back to enriched dioxide. All these processes are done in enclosed stainless steel vessels. The uranium compounds always have to be kept free of contamination. As in the mine, it is important to ensure that no one working in the plant breathes any of the powder or fumes. Because uranium is radioactive it is easy to keep a very sensitive check on leaks.

39

Above *'Magnox' fuel elements. Uranium metal rods are enclosed in magnesium alloy cans.*

Uranium fuel – metal

The refinery produces billets of uranium metal or uranium dioxide which is a black powder. The metal billets are re-melted into rough bars, and the bars are turned on lathes to accurate sizes to form fuel rods. These are about a metre (3·2 feet) long and about three centimetres (one inch) in diameter.

The designer of the reactor has calculated the size and arrangement of these pieces of fissile material which are needed to maintain the chain reaction. He has calculated the power which the uranium is to produce, and how hot it will get in doing so. The uranium, when the reactor is operating, will have fission products forming inside it. These are radioactive, and must be prevented from escaping and circulating in the coolant.

The uranium, if it was bare, would be corroded by the carbon dioxide coolant gas. To protect it, and to keep in the fission products, the rod has to be enclosed in a sealed "can". The can must let the heat produced by the rod pass freely to the coolant. When the coolant is a gas, as it is in the Magnox reactors, it helps to have fins on the outside of the cans. These make the gas eddy round them, and thus help to carry away the heat. The can has to be made of a material which does not absorb many neutrons. Magnesium is a good metal to use.

Above *Cleaning magnesium alloy swarf from the machine used for cutting the heat transfer surface on cans for 'Magnox' fuel.*

Uranium dioxide fuel

Uranium dioxide is a ceramic – a strong but brittle material. It cannot be machined like a metal. Instead it is made into a powder, pressed into shape, and "fired" in a furnace to produce hard black pellets. These fuel pellets are usually as long as your fingernail, and about the same in diameter. A rod would be brittle and crack too easily on handling. The pellets cannot be turned on a lathe, but they can be ground to an accurate size.

Uranium dioxide works at a higher temperature than uranium metal in the reactor. Magnesium cannot be used for the can – it would melt or corrode. Instead, stainless steel, or an alloy of a metal called zirconium is used. The cans which contain the elements for Advanced Gas-cooled Reactors (AGRs) are made from stainless steel like those used in fast reactors. Water and sodium do not require the surface of the can to have fins. The "heat transfer" to liquids is good, and the surfaces of the cans are therefore left smooth.

Left *Blenders used in the production of uranium oxide powder at the Springfields Works near Preston in England. Uranium dioxide powder is made into fuel pellets.*

Right *The fuel pellets are enclosed in stainless steel cans before being loaded into the fast reactor.*

Types of fuel elements

Above *Assembling a fast reactor fuel bundle.*

Fuel elements are made in many different shapes and sizes. The uranium metal fuel element, clad in magnesium alloy, is the fattest. The rod is usually about one metre (3·2 feet) long and about three centimetres (one inch) thick. The fuel elements containing uranium dioxide are thinner – the centre would get too hot if they were not. They are usually about 1 centimetre (0·4 inch) in diameter, but can be from one metre (3·2 feet) to four metres (13 feet) long. Each can contains many fuel pellets.

The cans are fastened together in bundles to make them easier to handle. Spacing devices keep them apart, so that the coolant can flow between them all, removing the heat. The bundles are often then referred to as the fuel elements. The individual fuelled cans are then called "fuel rods". Sometimes the bundle is enclosed inside a sleeve of metal or graphite.

Before a new type of fuel element is used in a reactor, it is given many tests in laboratories. It is heated to the temperature it will work at, in the substance to be used as coolant, at the working pressure. The properties of materials to be used are also very carefully studied. New alloys may be developed which have just the properties the designer of the fuel element wants.

Left *This type of fuel bundle is used in Canadian reactors.*

45

Sealing cans

The fuel element must be carefully sealed, to keep the fission products in and the coolant out. This sealing is usually done by welding on caps at each end of the can. A welding arc, which heats up the metal, is moved round the join. The metals of the can and the cap melt and run together, so that when they cool and solidify the join is completely sealed. This is done with an automatic machine so that the weld is as regular as possible.

The welds are then tested to make sure that they are not leaking. The space between the fuel and the can is filled with helium gas before the welds are made. Afterwards, the sealed fuel element is put into a test chamber from which all the air is pumped out. If there is a leak, the helium will start to escape into the vacuum in the test chamber. If any helium does, it is detected by a mass-spectrometer. This is a very sensitive instrument, connected to the test chamber, which is tuned to detect atoms of a particular element. A fuel element which is found to be leaking is rejected from the production line.

Right   *The final assembly and inspection of fuel pins during the manufacture of fuel elements.*

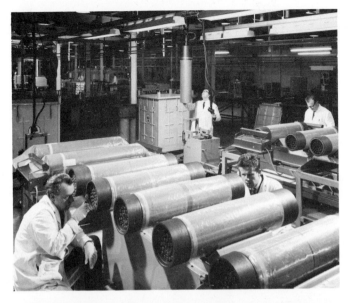

Inspection and testing

All the way through the manufacture of nuclear fuel you will find people inspecting, testing, and taking samples for analysis. The fuel and the can must be pure and free of any other substance which would absorb neutrons. The cans must also be without any flaw which might make them break or leak in service.

The metal tubing from which the can is to be made is inspected. The metal billet or ingot from which the tubing was made may itself have been inspected first. They are often inspected by using pulses of ultrasound – sound too high for our ears to hear. If there is a hole or a crack in the metal, an echo will come back to the ultrasonic testing unit. Fuel elements are often radiographed, too, to check that there are no hidden flaws.

Inspectors keep a constant check on the radiation levels for safety. Nuclear power is a new industry, and from the start people have realized the need to measure radiation levels. Perhaps because of this, and the attention paid to safety, there are fewer accidents and less sickness than in most other industries.

Top left *The visual inspection of pin location in an Advanced Gas-Cooled Reactor fuel element.*
Bottom left *Fuel pins are inspected at every stage of their manufacture.*

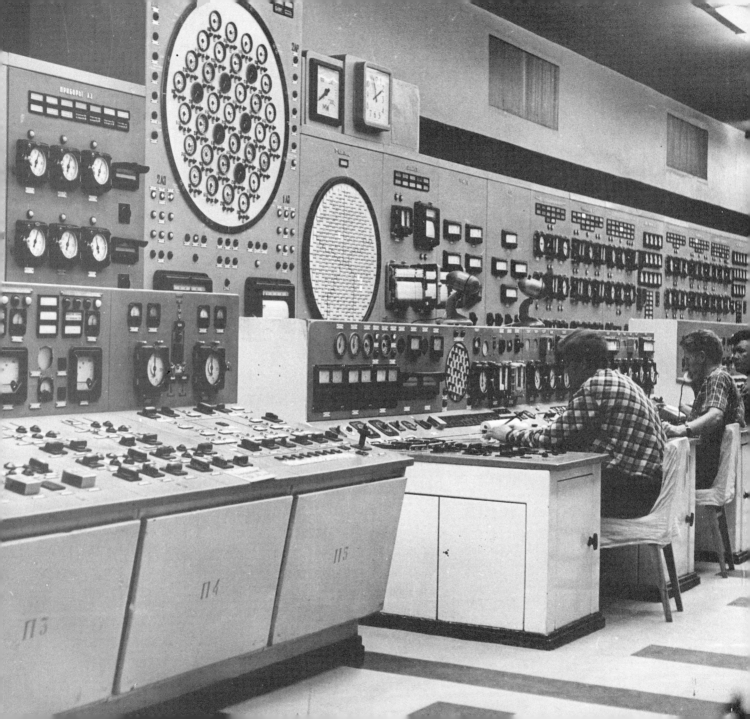

Operating a reactor

The engineers who operate a nuclear power reactor have the same tasks to do as those who operate other kinds of power station. Their instruments record the power at which the reactor is working, and also the pressures, temperatures and pumping rates in various parts of the plant. As much control as possible is automatic.

The power at which the reactor runs is usually kept steady. But the electric distribution system – "the grid" – into which the power is being fed may want more or less power. To match this, the power of the reactor is changed by moving the control rods in or out of the core. When the reactor needs to be shut down, the control rods are put all the way in.

There is more than one control system, with separate power supplies and drives, for safety. Water reactors have arrangements for adding substances such as boron to the water. These

Above *The control room at Hinkley B power station in England. Three computers are used, one for each reactor/turbine unit and one as an automatic standby for the station.*

substances absorb neutrons and serve much the same function as control rods. The level of radioactivity of the coolant is always measured. If this rises above a certain level, the reactor is shut down to check for faulty fuel elements.

Left *The control room of an atomic power station in the U.S.S.R.*

49

Fuelling the reactor

New fuel elements are not very radioactive. They can be safely transported to the reactor in ordinary steel boxes. One of the main differences between fuelling a nuclear power station and one burning fossil fuels is the amount of fuel needed. One tonne of uranium will produce more energy than ten thousand tonnes of coal. In the future, if it is "converted" in a fast reactor, it may produce more energy than half a million tonnes of coal. Even with present-day reactors, a power station can be kept fuelled by one lorry bringing fuel elements. A fossil fuelled power station needs train loads.

Some reactors can load and discharge fuel without needing to shut down. They can change fuel elements a few at a time. Others shut down perhaps once a year to discharge old fuel and load new. When fuel elements are to be loaded into the reactor they are unpacked from their transport boxes. They are inspected again to check that they are in a satisfactory condition for loading.

The reactor has a loading machine. The fuel elements are put into it, and they are loaded into the core of the reactor. Most reactors have vertical channels down which the fuel elements are lowered. The Canadian CANDU reactors, however, have horizontal channels into which the fuel elements are pushed.

Above   *A view inside one of the reactors at the Magnox power station at Wylfa in North Wales showing the fuelling machine in position on the pile cap floor. Fuelling operations can be carried out while the reactors are on full load.*

Above *A Canadian CANDU reactor fuelling while on power. This system also avoids the need for fuelling shutdowns so that the reactor can be available 100 per cent of the time.*

Discharging spent fuel

When a fuel element has been in the reactor for at least a year (it may be several years), its uranium 235 begins to be used up. The nuclear engineers say that its "fissile material" is being "burned up". As the amount of uranium 235 gets less, so the fission products build up. Each atom of uranium 235 which splits up, releasing energy, leaves two atoms in its place. Some of these atoms absorb neutrons, so that as time goes by, the fuel element becomes less reactive, and can release less energy. Eventually it is unloaded ("discharged") from the reactor and replaced with a new fuel element.

As the fuel element comes out of the reactor, it gives off a great amount of radiation. This is because of the fission products it contains. The discharge machine is similar to the charge machine which loaded the fuel element, except that it is shielded with heavy plates. These stop the radiation, and protect the operator of the machine and anyone else in that part of the reactor.

The "spent" fuel element is usually lowered and stored for a while in a deep pool of water –

Left *The charge/discharge machine in position on one of the pile caps at the AGR Hinkley Point power station near Bridgwater in Somerset, England.*

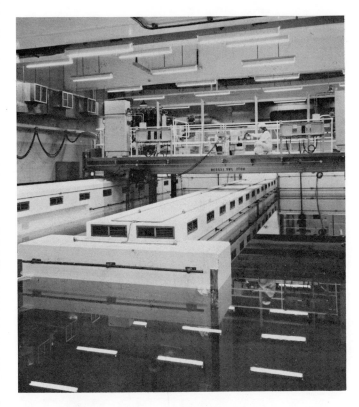

Above *The cooling pond – discharged fuel elements are stored in a pond for several months to allow the high intensity radiation to die down before they are dispatched for processing.*

Above *A Magnox fuel flask is removed from a power station in Suffolk, England. The flask absorbs the radiation from the fission products.*

the "pond". The fuel element continues to generate heat after it is taken out of the reactor. This heat comes from the radioactivity of the fission products. The heat falls off quite quickly with time, however.

When they are less radioactive, the fuel elements are taken for re-processing. They are transported in thick-walled steel vessels called "flasks". The flask absorbs the radiation from the fission products. It is also very strong, so that if anything collides with it, no dangerous material will be released.

53

Above *Post-irradiation examination at a laboratory in England. This lead shielded cell contains apparatus which uses a laser beam for the piercing of fuel cans.*

Post-irradiation examination

Some fuel elements are inspected after they have been discharged from the reactor. The designers and manufacturers want to check that the fuel elements have behaved as expected. After they have been in the reactor, the fuel elements are said to have been "irradiated".

Materials may change under irradiation. They may swell slightly and change their shapes. They may become more brittle than they were when new. By examining irradiated fuel elements, the engineers can often think of ways of improving the design.

To examine very radioactive objects you need to be able to see them and "handle" them without being exposed to the radiation they are giving off. To do this, the fuel elements are put inside "cells" with thick walls of lead or concrete. People outside can see them through thick windows. Mechanical "hands" have been designed and made so that by working controls outside the cell, objects can be lifted about inside. The fuel element can be moved about, weighed, measured, and cut up.

Practically any piece of laboratory equipment can be used inside the cell. Parts of the fuel and the can may be examined through the microscope, and quite complicated experiments are performed.

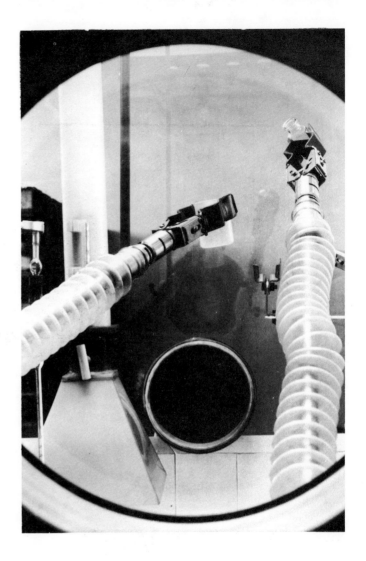

Above *Manipulators are used to 'handle' radioactive objects.*

55

Above *Irradiated fuel elements are remotely decanned under visual inspection inside thick walled concrete caves prior to reprocessing at the Windscale Works, in Cumbria, England.*

Re-processing fuel

The spent fuel could be stored in the pond for many years, but many nuclear power organizations prefer to "re-process" it. The fuel has four main ingredients. There is the non-fissile uranium 238, making up the greater part. There is the unburnt uranium 235. There is plutonium, which has been formed from uranium 238 absorbing neutrons. There are traces of other elements heavier than uranium, and finally there are the fission products. All these have their uses.

The uranium 235 can be made into fuel elements again. The plutonium can also be used as fuel, particularly for a fast reactor. The uranium 238 can be converted into plutonium by a fast reactor. Some fission products can be used in industry and in scientific and medical research. There are many uses for radioisotopes, as they are called – they would fill a book of their own. But most fission products will probably not be used in this way. They are considered wastes, like the ashes from furnaces, and like ashes they must be disposed of where they can do no harm.

In re-processing, the fuel element is taken apart again. The operators work from behind shielding to protect themselves from the radioactivity of the spent fuel. The cans are stripped off. The fuel is chopped up into pieces

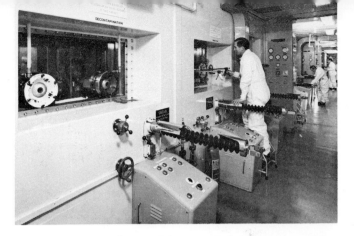

Above　*The manufacture of plutonium fuel. Operators work from behind shielding to protect themselves from the radioactivity of the spent fuel.*

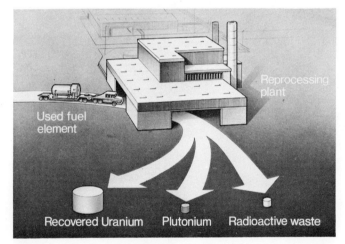

Recovered Uranium　　Plutonium　　Radioactive waste

Above　*The reprocessing stream.*

and dissolved in acid. Then, by chemical treatment, the uranium, plutonium and fission products are separated.

57

Storage of fission products

Though nuclear power stations have been operating since the 1950s, the amount of fission products from spent fuel is still small. All the fission products from the nuclear energy generated so far in Britain are stored in solution in stainless steel tanks. These tanks are a small part of the fuel re-processing factory at Windscale in Cumbria. However, as we are

Below *Glass filled stainless steel cylinders are stored in special ponds.*

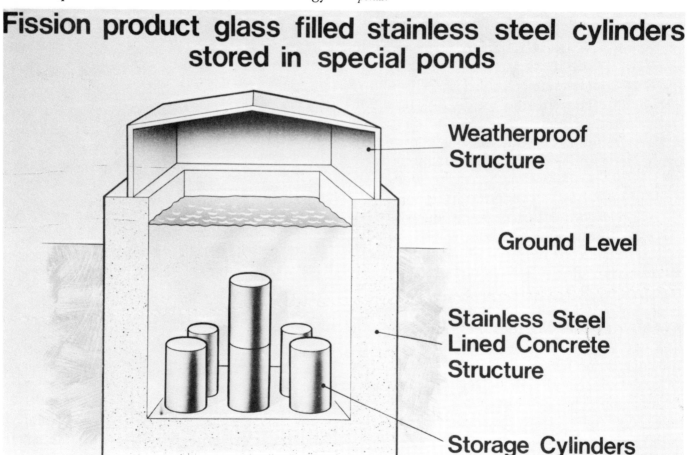

Fission product glass filled stainless steel cylinders stored in special ponds

Weatherproof Structure

Ground Level

Stainless Steel Lined Concrete Structure

Storage Cylinders

using more energy from nuclear power stations year by year, it is sensible to think about permanent storage. One way which will probably be used is to mix the fission products into a solid mass of glass. The glass will be solidified inside steel vessels, which would be sealed up. These containers could then be stored underground, so that the radiation could not reach the surface.

Many people misunderstand the extent to which the fission products remain radioactive. A radioactive element "decays" at a decreasing rate. Scientists talk about its "half-life". If it has a half-life of ten years, this means that after ten years, half the atoms have stopped being radioactive. After twenty years, only a quarter are active, after thirty years only an eighth are, and so on. The high activity of spent fuel when it comes out of the reactor comes from the fission products with short half-lives. There are fission products with long half-lives, but not very many of them. After a few hundred years the glass blocks will be no more radioactive than many natural minerals.

Above *If all the electric power, both domestic and industrial, that one man used in his lifetime were generated by nuclear power alone, the long lived radioactive wastes that would be produced could all be incorporated in a piece of glass this size.*

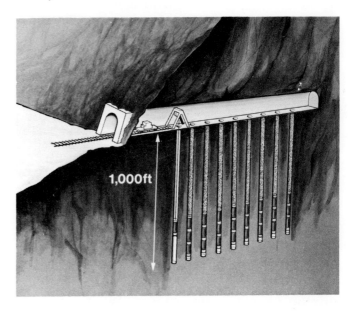

1,000ft

Above *A diagram showing a possible way of disposing of highly active waste by burial in deep, stable, geological formations.*

Pollution and safety

During the twentieth century, people have realized the dangers of pollution. This is partly because we now know more about the effects of smoke and other waste products upon living things. We know, for example, that many substances can cause cancer and other diseases, and should be avoided. We also have very sensitive apparatus for analysing so that we can detect very small traces of chemicals in air, water, and living things.

Radioactivity can be harmful, so we should be concerned about radioactive pollution. Fortunately radioactivity can be very easily and sensitively measured. Everything about us is naturally radioactive, including our own bodies. This is because there are natural radioactive elements.

There are uranium and thorium in the earth and in the sea. There is about three thousandths of a gramme of uranium in every cubic metre of sea-water, so that the oceans contain thousands of millions of tons of uranium. There is radioactive potassium mixed in with the inactive potassium in many substances, including our bodies.

Radioactive elements, like many other substances, can cause cancer. What we must decide is how low the radioactive levels from our own operations like nuclear power should be kept. The problem is the same as how to make sure the air is clean in towns. No-one can do away with burning things altogether, but we can keep down smoke to a low level.

Below *A 'tacky shade' collector is a device which monitors radiation. Two wire frames are covered with a tacky gauze-like material to which airborne particles stick.*

The place of nuclear energy

The modern technical society we live in uses large amounts of energy. Some people say that we use too much. But not many people would prefer to return to a way of life where your power was limited to your own effort, or your servants', or your slaves'. (You might turn out to be one of the servants instead of the rich man he waited on!)

Modern industrial society was first built up using coal to fire its steam engines. Today, most of our engines run on oil. But there is only a limited amount of oil in the world. There are greater coal reserves, so countries may return to that source for the energy they require. The miners who dig it however, should have better and safer working conditions than they have at present. This may make coal very expensive.

There is still enough coal and oil in the world. But if the poorer countries of the world used energy at the same rate as the developed countries – those in North America, Europe, Russia and Australasia – the coal and oil reserves would soon be used up. It would be wrong to stop the poorer countries from advancing

Below *This water wheel on the Isle of Man was one of the earliest constructions built to generate power from water on a large scale.*

Above *Solar energy will almost certainly be used to a much greater extent in countries where there is strong, consistent sunshine. Here we see a commercial type of solar cooker being demonstrated in New Delhi, India.*

technically, as they must do to better the lives of their peoples. So where will we find enough energy to ensure that the whole world is more prosperous? What other sources of energy might we use?

Hydro-power from the rivers, and tidal power from the seas are practicable, but there is only a limited amount of energy that can be obtained from them. Solar energy, and energy from the wind and waves may help us in the future. Solar energy will almost certainly be used to a greater extent, particularly in countries where there is strong, steady sunshine.

We may find ways of harnessing these "alternative sources" cheaply and reliably. If we do so, nuclear energy may diminish in importance in the same way that coal burning has done. Fusion energy may become available, though not until the twenty first century, as we do not know how to harness it yet. Prophecies are risky in science and technology, but it is probable that fission energy will be an important source during the next fifty years at least, and probably for longer.

It will be particularly useful for countries without coal, oil or gas. It may tend to be first used in those countries which already have industries to power, and an electrical "grid" to distribute the power generated. But any country using nuclear energy is making it easier for other countries to get coal and oil.

Reactors in ships

When steam engines were invented, one use they were soon put to was driving ships. When nuclear powered reactors were built, engineers realized that a ship could be driven by turbines worked by steam coming from a reactor. A nuclear-powered ship can travel long distances before it needs to refuel. This is valuable for a fighting ship, and the navies of the USA, the Soviet Union, Great Britain and France now

Above *This nuclear-powered submarine can cruise for great distances without having to refuel.*

Above *As soon as steam engines were invented they were used to power ships.*

have nuclear-powered vessels. The Soviet Union also has nuclear-powered ice-breakers. In the USA, Germany and Japan, experimental nuclear cargo ships have been built. So far they have proved to be more expensive to run than oil-fired ships, and no more are planned. If oil becomes scarce, as it must sooner or later, we may see more nuclear-powered merchant ships.

63

Fusion energy

People have always wondered how the Sun keeps "burning". If it were burning chemically, like a fire, no fuel could have kept it going for the thousands of millions of years for which it has probably existed. This puzzled scientists before nuclear theory was developed, but we can see now that the Sun, and the other stars, get their energy by converting hydrogen into helium.

We have already made "fusion" happen as an explosion in the hydrogen bomb. It is more difficult to make it happen in a slow, controlled way in a fusion reactor for a power station. We need to produce temperatures of millions of degrees to make hydrogen atoms fuse together.

Making machines to contain the very hot gases is the central problem of fusion research. A fusion reactor will either have strong magnetic fields to hold the hot gases, or perhaps use powerful lasers to heat up the fuel suddenly. The energy it produces is not likely to be cheaper than that from any other source. There should however be no fuel problem if we can "fusion-burn" hydrogen from the water of the sea!

Right *The Sun (here seen in eclipse) and other stars keep burning by converting hydrogen into helium.*

Objections to nuclear energy

Some people would prefer that nuclear energy was not used at all. They say:

"Nuclear power stations release radioactive substances."

So they do, but in very small amounts. Burning coal in a power station may release more. There is radioactivity from natural material all around us; the amount released from power stations is tiny in comparison. They also think it possible that:

"A nuclear power station may have an accident and release much more radioactivity than usual."

This is possible, but very improbable. A reactor cannot explode like a bomb – it is too "spread out" for that. The worst accident for a reactor would be for it to get too hot. If this happened the fuel elements might fail, and release radioactive material into the coolant. The pressure vessel holding the coolant, and the building containing it, would both have to fail before the material escaped. The designers of a reactor set out to make all these events very unlikely. Their designs are also examined by a separate team of engineers and scientists whose job is to check for safety.

Right   *The face of protest.*

Nuclear explosives

Nuclear fission was first used by man to make bombs. The use of knowledge to create violence and destruction is common in history. To make better swords and armour, smiths improved both the ways of making steel and the methods of working it. Soon after the aeroplane was invented it was turned into a fighting machine, and man's knowledge of aeronautics was greatly improved.

Nuclear energy is associated in many peoples' minds with its first use – to destroy the Japanese cities of Hiroshima and Nagasaki in 1945. The main release of radioactivity to the environment was through the testing of bombs, which went on throughout the 1950s and 1960s. This "bomb testing" has now virtually stopped through international agreement, and "nuclear fallout" is steadily getting less.

It is the fear of radioactivity being leaked into the environment which has led some people to oppose nuclear energy. Another fear is that fissile material might be stolen and made into explosives.

Six governments in the world have made nuclear explosives already. If we are to make sure that they are never used, we must do so by international action. We know about fission, and the knowledge cannot be kept quiet. One way to prevent powerful weapons from being

Above *A 'mushroom cloud' billows high above Nagasaki after the second atomic bomb had been dropped on Japan in 1945.*

used is to seek to avoid war and violence by removing their causes. The best way to a peaceful world may be through prosperity. For that we need energy.

66

Nuclear energy – past, present, and future

Nuclear energy has been at our disposal only since 1942. This is a very short time in the history of mankind. Nuclear fuel is a new kind of fuel – the discovery of a "new" fire. It is now an established source of energy in many countries, and is likely to be more widely used in the future. How much the use of nuclear fuel will grow in the next few years will depend on many factors. The most important of these is probably how the nations producing oil decide to sell it to the rest of the world. But whatever the price of oil, it must start to become scarce during the next hundred years. Those of us who work in nuclear energy, and many other people too, think that nuclear energy is needed. We think that it is needed now, and will be needed along with the other sources of energy, as far ahead as we can see. You, the reader of this book, must judge for yourself.

Above *Oil, the fuel of the past?*

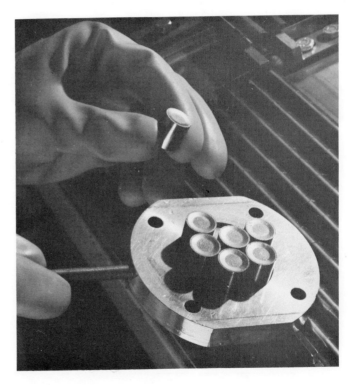

Above *Nuclear fuel pellets – the fuel of the future?*

67

Facts and figures

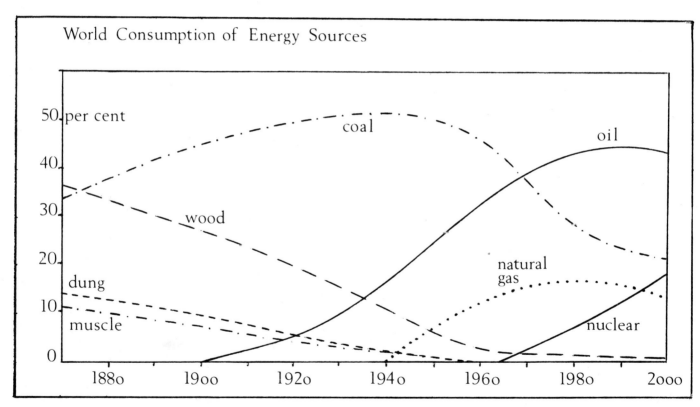

World Consumption of Energy Sources

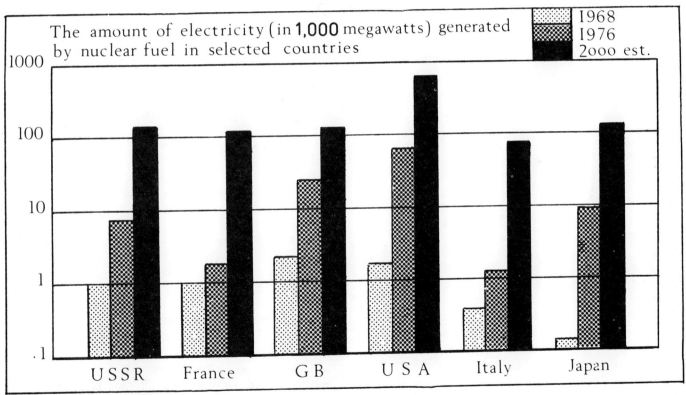

The amount of electricity (in **1,000** megawatts) generated by nuclear fuel in selected countries

1968
1976
2ooo est.

1000

100

10

1

.1

USSR   France   G B   U S A   Italy   Japan

Glossary

AGR Advanced Gas-Cooled Reactor. A design of reactor using fuel elements of uranium dioxide clad in stainless steel, with graphite moderator and cooled by carbon dioxide gas.

Atom The smallest portion into which an element can be divided.

BWR Boiling Water Reactor. A design of reactor using fuel elements of uranium dioxide clad in stainless steel or zirconium alloy cooled by water which boils as it passes through the core.

Ceramic An oxide, or other compound of a metal, which is hard and brittle and has a high melting-point.

Depleted Uranium Uranium which contains less than the normal amount of the U^{235} isotope.

Element A distinct kind of atom. There are about a hundred different kinds, and these elements make up all known matter.

Energy The ability to do work, or cause things to change.

Enriched Uranium Uranium which contains more than the normal amount of the U^{235} isotope.

Fast Reactor A reactor with no moderator, so that the neutrons given off in fission are not slowed down.

Fissile Capable of undergoing fission.

Fission The splitting of the nucleus of an atom into two parts, making two new atoms.

Fission Product A new atom produced by fission.

Fossil Fuel Coal, oil and natural gas, the remains of long-dead plants or animals.

Fuel Anything which can be burned or consumed to release energy.

Fuel Element Fissile material enclosed in protective cladding ('can') for loading into a reactor.

Fusion Building up a heavier atom from lighter ones.

Isotopes Different forms of the same element. The nuclei have the same numbers of protons in them, but different numbers of neutrons, so that they have different weights.

Magnox Reactor A design of reactor using fuel elements of uranium metal clad in Magnox (an alloy of magnesium) with graphite moderator and cooled by carbon dioxide gas.

Molecule A group of two or more atoms, of the same element or of different elements, joined together to form the smallest part of a substance that can exist.

Natural Uranium Uranium as it is found in the earth, which has not been enriched or depleted.

Neutron A basic particle occurring in all atomic nuclei. It has no electric charge, and so can enter the nuclei of atoms easily. It takes part in the chain reaction which releases energy in nuclear reactors.

Nuclear Fuel Uranium or plutonium, purified and

made into fuel elements for nuclear reactors.

Nucleus The central part of an atom, made up of protons and neutrons and containing most of its mass.

Plutonium A heavier element than uranium, produced in a reactor by neutrons entering the nuclei of uranium atoms.

Power The rate at which energy is released.

PWR Pressurised Water Reactor. A design of reactor using fuel elements of uranium dioxide clad in stainless steel or zirconium alloy cooled by water held under high pressure to prevent it boiling.

Radioactivity The way in which some atoms change ('decay') by sending out particles or rays ('radiation')

Radioisotope An isotope which is radioactive. Those which are not are called 'stable isotopes'.

Reactor An assembly of fissile material, in the form of nuclear fuel, which can be made to sustain a chain-reaction of fission and release energy.

Thermal Reactor A reactor where the neutrons from fission are slowed down by moderating material so that the chain-reaction can go ahead more easily.

Acknowledgements

The author and publishers would like to thank those who gave permission for their illustrations to appear on the following pages: British Nuclear Fuels, 40, 42, 43, 46, 58; Canada House, 6, 11, 33, 36a, 36b, 37, 44, 51; Central Electricity Generating Board, Cover, 7, 29, 32, 49, 50, 52, 53a, 53b, 60; Graham Rickard, 8, 10, 13b, 17, 24, 25; High Commission for New Zealand, 14, 15; International Atomic Energy Agency, 55; Johnson Matthey Group, 19b; Society for Cultural Relations with the U.S.S.R., 31. 48; United Kingdom Atomic Energy Authority, 21a, 21b, 23, 26, 28, 30, 34, 35, 38, 39, 41, 45, 47a, 47b, 54, 56, 57a, 57b, 59a, 59b, 67b. All other pictures are from the Wayland Picture Library.

Index